Houses & Homes

Carolyn Cocke

Macdonald Educational

Editor Kate Woodhouse
Assistant Editor Caroline Russum
Design Arthur Lockwood
Production Philip Hughes
Picture Research Mary Walsh

First published 1976

Macdonald Educational Ltd
Holywell House
Worship Street
London EC2A 2EN

contents

ISBN 0 356 05461 6

© Macdonald Educational Ltd 1976

Printed in Belgium by H. PROOST & Cie p.v.b.a.

The need for shelter

▲ The people living in this village on stilts in Thailand have two sources of food. The land has been flooded for growing rice and fish can be caught in the nearby rivers.

◄ This very simple African Kirdi shelter of wood and grass will protect its occupants from the tropical sun and heat.

▼ This castle offered protection to its residents and to the peasants living in the neighbouring village. When enemy soldiers approached, people would run into the castle and the drawbridge would be drawn up after them.

Shelter, food and defence

Shelter, together with food and clothing, is one of the basic human needs. There are very few parts of the world where people can live without shelter. People need shelter to take cover when the weather is bad, and as a place to sleep at night. If people have no shelter, they have to spend so much energy just keeping alive that they have no time to do anything else.

One of the reasons people chose a particular place to build shelter was to be near a source of food. Even today it is more convenient to live near shops. Protection from enemies, both animals and humans, is a further reason for shelter. Nowadays, in most places, it is not necessary to defend each house separately, but in times of danger people strengthen their houses to keep enemies out.

What is a home?

More than a shelter

People need houses to shelter from bad weather or from danger, but these needs are so obvious and so basic that most of the time people don't even think about them. When it is raining, you don't think of home as somewhere to go to get out of the rain—a bus shelter would do as well. Instead, you think of home as the place where you can find dry clothes to change into, or where you can do something else until the rain has stopped. Although we cannot do without it, it is not the shelter a house gives that makes it important to us. What is it, all over the world, that makes people fond of their homes?

A haven of safety

One answer is that houses give us a feeling of safety. We need to feel safe—to have a place to hide—as much as we need the protection of walls and a roof.

Home, too, is a place of shelter for growing up in. Animals build nests or homes for this reason, but they do not generally need permanent structures because their young can learn to fend for themselves in quite a short time. Human children on the other hand often need the shelter of home long after they are physically able to do a day's work.

Of course homes are not only to do with feeling safe. A home is a place for doing many different things. As soon as someone moves in, the empty shell of a house becomes a home where people can eat, sleep, play, work, have their friends round, keep their possessions, and shut the door if they want to.

▲ This doll's house is an exact copy of a house built about two hundred years ago. The furniture and people are precisely as they would have been at that time. If you were to move into a house like this you would probably furnish and decorate it very differently.

◀ Most children enjoy playing at houses, building them out of old furniture or from natural materials like wood. Maybe we are all born with an instinct to build homes and mark out our own territories.

◀ San Marino in Italy was originally built as a haven against bandits in the plains below. Now, tourists like the picturesque views from the mountaintop homes.

▲ Caves need not necessarily be primitive! These ones in the Loire valley in France were first inhabited centuries ago, and have been adapted for modern life.

Natural homes

Animals also need a home. Some such as snails carry their own home around with them; others build a strong weather-proof shelter, or mark out a special territory for themselves.

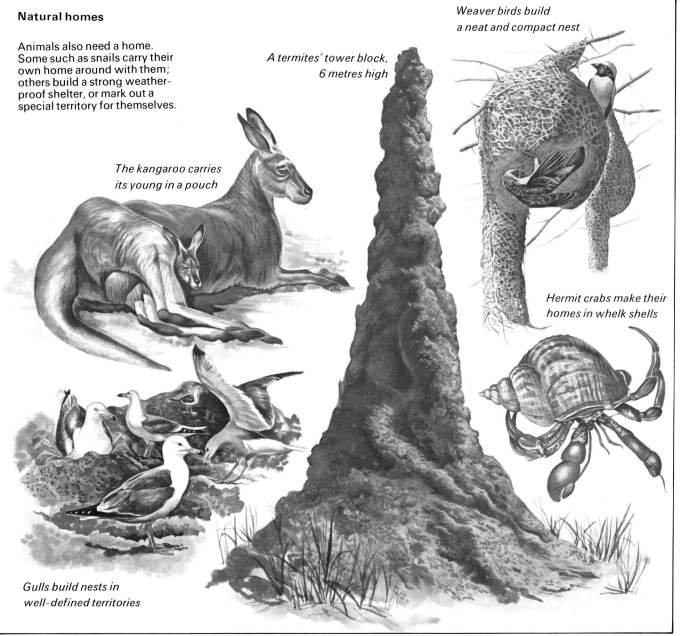

A termites' tower block, 6 metres high

Weaver birds build a neat and compact nest

The kangaroo carries its young in a pouch

Hermit crabs make their homes in whelk shells

Gulls build nests in well-defined territories

Climate a decisive factor

▲ An early form of air conditioning. This house in Bahrain, in the hot deserts of the Middle East, has a wind tower positioned to trap any breeze. The breeze is then channelled down into the house below as cooling air. The temperature in the house can reach as much as 55°C on a really hot day so even the slightest breeze is very welcome.

▲ At night, these courtyard houses in Morocco radiate the heat in their walls to the night sky. A pool of cool air is built up in the ground-floor rooms and the courtyard. This cool air should keep out the heat for a large part of the day. A fountain in the courtyard helps to keep the air cool, as you can see from the diagram on the right.

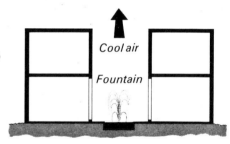

► The occupants of this house in tropical northern Australia are trying to make it as airy as possible. Louvred windows on all sides give plenty of draughts, keeping both the house and its occupants cool. The overhanging roof provides a shady outside sitting area. The diagram below shows the principle on which the house is built: to create as much of a through-current of air as possible.

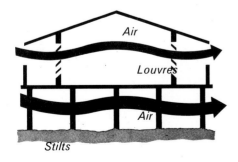

How to make an igloo

Firmly packed, even snow is best for the building blocks of an igloo. Three blocks on the round foundation are cut into a ramp so that the walls will continue in a spiral. Each layer is leaned slightly further inwards. When the king block, cut to fit, is lowered into the hole at the top, the cracks are filled with snow. Finally the underground tunnel entrance is made. It has two advantages: cold air cannot blow inside, and a pool of cool air remains low in the tunnel while the inside is heated by a small blubber-oil lamp. A hole must be left for ventilation.

The influence of climate

In most parts of the world the design and materials of houses depend on the climate. People living in hot countries, for example, want their houses to be as cool as possible. The building of houses to suit certain climates has meant that across the world the style of houses varies.

Many of these different designs have evolved through trial and error, but the principles of the building can often be proved scientifically correct. For example, many of the houses in tropical Africa have thick walls with small windows. The thick walls mean that it is difficult for the sun's heat to penetrate the walls, so that the interior stays cool. The same principles are used in colder countries, where the thick walls prevent any heat inside the house from escaping.

Roofs and heating

The design of the roof of a house can be as important as the walls and windows. In places where there is a great deal of rain or snow the roofs have to be "pitched" or sloped to carry the snow and rain away. In some countries the roofs slope gently so that snow can lie on the house to insulate it during the winter months. In hot countries where there is little rainfall, flat roofs are common and can be used as an extra room in the evening when the sun has gone down.

The invention of more efficient heating systems and air conditioning has meant that it is possible to standardize the materials and design of houses, but with the rising cost of fuel this may not continue. Houses may once again be built according to the climate.

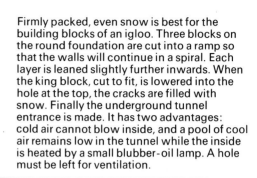

▲ Until recently no-one has been able to live in Antarctica. It has a much colder climate than the Arctic because the land mass is covered with a layer of ice up to 1800 metres thick. Modern technology provides heating for research stations where scientists studying the Antarctic can find shelter.

Preventing damp

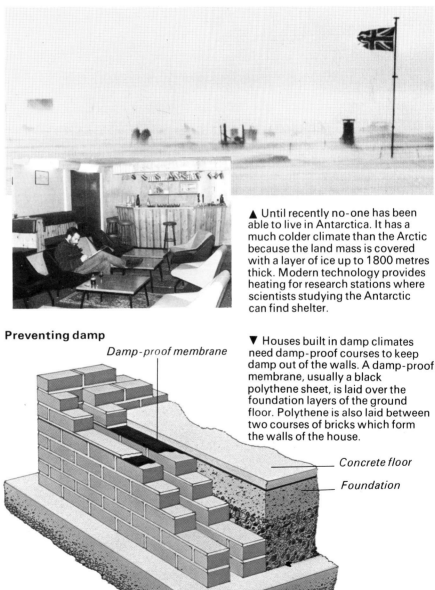

Damp-proof membrane

▼ Houses built in damp climates need damp-proof courses to keep damp out of the walls. A damp-proof membrane, usually a black polythene sheet, is laid over the foundation layers of the ground floor. Polythene is also laid between two courses of bricks which form the walls of the house.

Concrete floor

Foundation

Traditional building materials

Materials around us

People have used the natural materials around them to build their houses for thousands of years. Mud, vegetation, stone and wood are all traditional house-building materials, and have been used all over the world.

"Mud" is rather a misleading term for what are really dried-earth houses. The earth is usually gathered as mud, but only when it has dried out is it firm and strong enough to act as the walls of a house. Sometimes it is mixed with straw or stones to make it stronger. In dry parts of the world where there is no mud, earth is rammed in a mould and pounded until it forms a hard mass. Grasses, bamboos and reeds are some of the forms of vegetation used to build houses. They can be woven, plaited or used as thatch. Stone is an excellent building material, but is difficult to transport. Wood is another very good material, but not many areas can provide enough for building houses.

Bricks

A shortage of wood was one of the reasons for the development and greater use of bricks. Bricks were first made by the Romans, over two thousand years ago. Bricks are made from clay mixed with small pieces of stone and other

strengthening materials, which are then baked together at an extremely high temperature. The different colours in bricks come from the minerals in the earth used. Iron in the earth produces red bricks, yellow bricks contain lime or sulphur. Bricks are one of the most used of the traditional house-building materials as they are easy and cheap to make.

▲ This mud hut has been built in northern Ghana in Africa. The walls are made of mud, with tin plates inlaid round the doorway for decoration. The roof is made from grasses, laid on a wooden frame. The house has no window, so that it keeps as cool as possible.

▲ In some areas of Africa complete wood frames are made for houses. Bamboo and long grasses are then threaded and woven round the frame to make a light, flexible and airy house.

▶ Some African soils are particularly good for making mud houses, as they set rock-hard and may last for centuries. The curved surfaces of this house in Mali make it stronger than would sharp corners.

Timber frame

Daub

Split hazel twigs

▲ "Wattle and daub" was often used to fill the spaces between the load-bearing posts of a house's frame. Short poles were fitted into holes in the main timber and split twigs woven between them. This process was similar to the weaving of the African hut shown on the opposite page (bottom left), but to prevent cold air entering the house, the twigs were smeared with clay. Sometimes the walls would then be plastered.

A house built with natural materials

Bricks for chimney

Stone fireplace

Wood panelling

Window with small leaded panes

Plaster

Window without glass

Stone foundation

Timber framework

► This 16th-century house is built completely from local materials. Set on a foundation of stone, it has a wood frame, filled in with wattle and daub. Bricks have been used for the chimney since they are fire resistant. The bricks have not been plastered as they are a sign of wealth.

▼ This Australian house is built completely of wood, in the style of Canadian houses. It was hurriedly erected during the gold rush of the 1870s when houses sprang up almost overnight.

▼ These Scandinavian houses have roofs covered with growing turf. This is a form of thatching that will keep the house both warm and dry.

Craftsmanship

▲ The building of the Tower of Babel, as depicted by a 17th-century Dutchman. This stained-glass window reveals a great deal about the building techniques used in Holland in the 17th century. Many of the tools are similar to those used today. Notice the wooden ladders and the way in which building materials are being pulled up in a bucket.

▼ The marshmen of southern Iraq build remarkable dwellings with the reeds found there which can grow up to 7 metres high. The reeds are bound into long tapering pillars and set into holes in the ground. Two opposite pillars are then spliced and bound on together with rope. The row of hoops are made into a framework by fixing sticks between them, parallel to the ground. The framework is covered with matting.

Experts in using tools

One of the first great steps forward in the history of early man took place when he started to use tools. He discovered how to chip flints to make axes and knives. With these tools he could chop down trees and make a home out of wood.

People who are expert with tools are called craftsmen. Throughout the ages and all over the world people have been developing the skills of craftsmanship.

Wood, brick and stone are found in many places. Craftsmen who know how to use these materials, the carpenters, bricklayers and stonemasons, build houses that are similar, in places that may be great distances apart. But although the basic structure of houses may be the same, there is often a local way of decorating houses.

Learning the trade

The traditional way of learning a craftsman's trade was by the system of apprenticeship. The young apprentice did not learn his trade by going to school but by doing the job and watching how his master used his tools.

Today things are rather different. In these days of mass production there is little demand for the time-consuming crafts of thatching or woodcarving. People can no longer afford to pay for such workmanship. But experts such as carpenters, bricklayers, plasterers, plumbers and electricians are still needed. Many of their tools are powered by electricity. They still become apprentices but also spend time at technical colleges and schools where they learn the skills necessary for building the kind of homes we live in today.

Thatching

The straw is tied into bundles, and fixed on to the roof timbers with an iron spike. The thatcher works upwards from the lower edge of the roof, so that the bundles overlap and rain cannot seep in. He pats the thatch into place with a "leggat". The ridge of the roof is finished with bundles laid sideways and a pattern made along it with a trimming knife. Wire netting fastens the whole roof down.

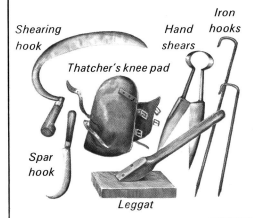

Shearing hook

Hand shears

Iron hooks

Thatcher's knee pad

Spar hook

Leggat

The first layer of thatch is laid.

The second layer of thatch.

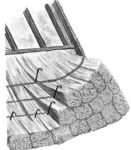

The third layer. Note the iron hooks keeping the thatch in place.

Bunches of thatch are laid along the ridge of the roof.

Thatching the eaves.

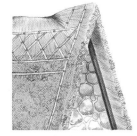

The finished roof with trimmed thatch.

▶ The variety of pattern in brick or stone can be endless. This house near Hamburg in Germany has a different pattern of brickwork in every panel.

The examples of stonework on the far right show just some of the diversity that can be achieved.

Modern building methods

Building with concrete

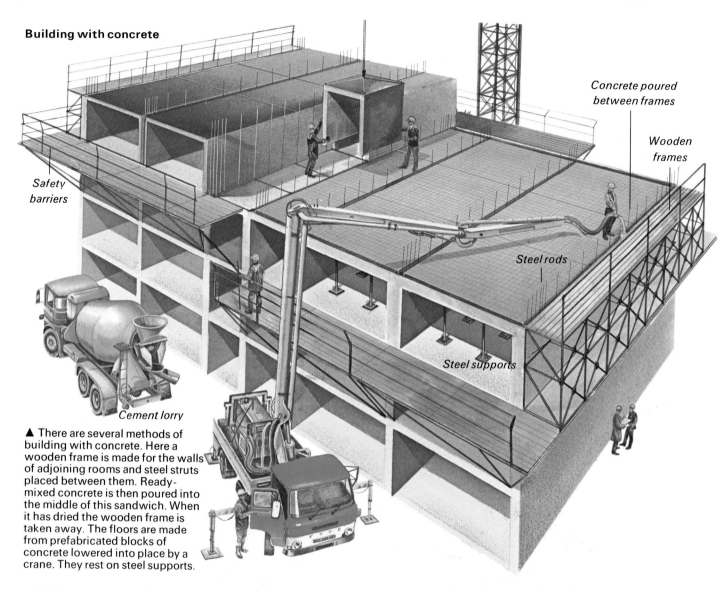

Concrete poured
between frames

Wooden
frames

Safety
barriers

Steel rods

Steel supports

Cement lorry

▲ There are several methods of
building with concrete. Here a
wooden frame is made for the walls
of adjoining rooms and steel struts
placed between them. Ready-
mixed concrete is then poured into
the middle of this sandwich. When
it has dried the wooden frame is
taken away. The floors are made
from prefabricated blocks of
concrete lowered into place by a
crane. They rest on steel supports.

▲ A house designed to be built from concrete.
It is difficult to add individual features to a
concrete house, but this one has an unusual
shape that would be impossible to build
in brick.

▲ A Canadian block of flats or a pile of
boxes? Again, this shape could not be
achieved with traditional materials; only
concrete enables flats to be built on thin air,
with apparently no support from below.

Concrete and plate glass

From the middle of the last century, builders began to use many new materials in addition to the traditional ones. The new materials made new methods of building possible. Concrete can be made into a solid wall, whereas bricks have to be laid layer by layer, or it can be made into beams longer and stronger than any wooden one. One result of these new materials is that houses today can look quite different to those of a hundred years ago.

Concrete, as we know it today, and plate glass were both products of the 19th century. Concrete is cheap to produce, very strong and resists fire, water and weather well. Plate glass can be made in sheets to fit large windows, so that rooms can become much more light and airy.

At the same time as the new materials were coming into use, transport was becoming cheaper. It was no use having a good new material if it could not be widely used. At one time the only way of transporting materials was by road or by sea, which was very expensive. So houses were generally built of materials found locally. After the invention of canals and railways the expense was less of a problem.

New methods, new shapes

Concrete and plate glass have made it possible to build large blocks of flats. The concrete can either be mixed on site, or the slabs that make up the walls can be made in a factory. This system is known as industrialized building because it brings some of the mass-production methods used in factories to the building trade.

How cement is made

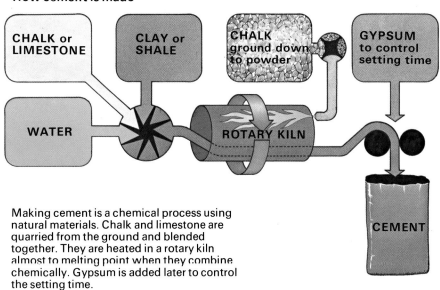

Making cement is a chemical process using natural materials. Chalk and limestone are quarried from the ground and blended together. They are heated in a rotary kiln almost to melting point when they combine chemically. Gypsum is added later to control the setting time.

How concrete works

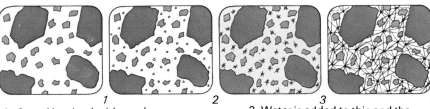

1. Gravel is mixed with sand.
2. Cement powder is poured into the mixture and fills the space between the gravel and sand.
3. Water is added to this and the cement starts to grow into crystals.
4. The crystals grow to bind the sand and gravel together into a solid mass.

◀ From a hole in the ground to a house in four hours. The four sections of this house were built in a factory and transported to the site when they were complete. Building like this means that no time is lost through bad weather, a great advantage in some countries.

▲ "You'd better get washed and changed. They're having company." One of the disadvantages of large, plate-glass windows can be the lack of privacy if you are overlooked, but they do give plenty of light and an impression of space.

Making a house work

Garderobe

History of the lavatory

The present-day flush lavatory is a comparatively modern invention. Five hundred years ago the garderobe was just a hole which emptied on to the ground below. The water closet was invented 150 years ago, and even today many people do not have one in their home.

19th-century water closet

Necessities of a house

It is not enough for people just to have a roof over their heads. They have to have water for drinking, cooking and washing. They need some way of lighting a house when it is dark, and in cold climates some form of heating is essential.

In the past when most people lived in the country, they had to get all the water and fuel they needed for their houses themselves. Houses were built where there was a good supply of water and fuel, as well as food.

Nowadays it is not possible for people in towns to go out and look for water and fuel. It would also be a waste of time. It is much more practical for the authorities to provide a central service to each house of water, gas and electricity. These services provide homes with all the basic necessities. The telephone and rubbish collection are additional central services.

Essential services

The ancient Romans understood the need for central services very well when they built their first cities. They built huge aqueducts to bring in clean water from far away. Nowadays great care is taken to ensure that the water supply to towns is clean enough to drink, and that sewage is purified before being returned to the rivers.

Until recently all houses were heated by burning fuel in a stove or fireplace. Modern systems of heating, using electricity, gas or oil, have the advantage that they can be controlled very easily, at the touch of a switch. In the future, as fuel becomes scarce and expensive, new and economical ways of heating houses will have to be developed. The whole of a district in a town may have heat piped to its houses from a central source. This means that we may soon have further services centrally supplied.

▶ An old-fashioned kitchen. The kitchen used to be the most important room in the house. The range which you can see in the background was often the only heating in the house, and was used for cooking, drying and heating. Many houses later installed a gas cooker to supplement the range.

▼ The modern kitchen looks quite different — with its shiny surfaces and electric gadgets. Although not as cosy, it is still a very important part of the home, where people eat, talk and play.

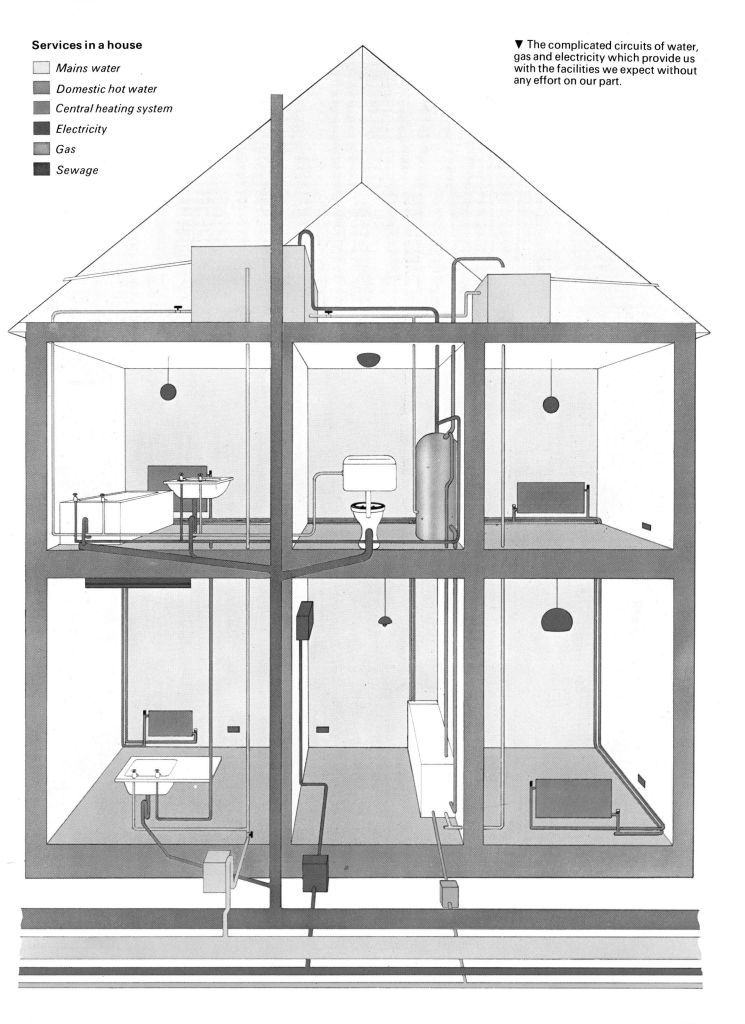

Services in a house

- Mains water
- Domestic hot water
- Central heating system
- Electricity
- Gas
- Sewage

▼ The complicated circuits of water, gas and electricity which provide us with the facilities we expect without any effort on our part.

Using a home

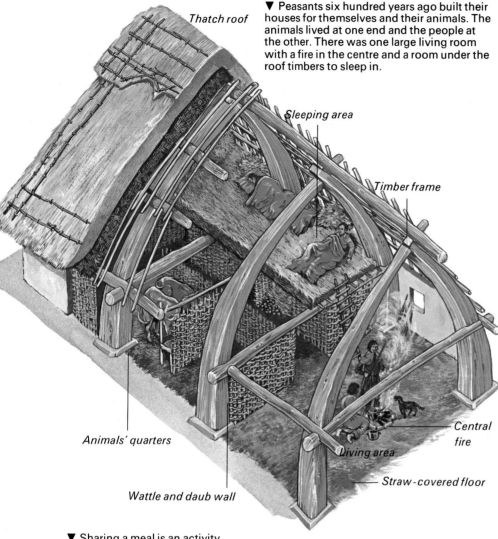

Thatch roof

▼ Peasants six hundred years ago built their houses for themselves and their animals. The animals lived at one end and the people at the other. There was one large living room with a fire in the centre and a room under the roof timbers to sleep in.

Sleeping area

Timber frame

Animals' quarters

Central fire

Living area

Straw-covered floor

Wattle and daub wall

▼ Sharing a meal is an activity which happens in houses all over the world. Although the way in which it is done may vary from country to country, mealtimes everywhere are an opportunity for members of a family to come together.

Activities indoors

We hardly ever think about the basic reason for needing a house, which is to provide shelter, because all the other activities that take place there are so important to us. Whatever the design or materials of a house, it is what goes on inside that matters most.

Community and privacy

Some family activities, like meals, take place with everyone together, but many people consider that privacy is also necessary. This is a fairly new idea. Five hundred years ago everyone living in a castle would have shared the main hall for eating, sleeping and working. It was not until the second half of the 16th century when corridors were invented that rooms became private. Before that one room opened into another so people were still really living as a community and had very little privacy.

A hundred and fifty years ago most houses did not have a particular use fixed for each room. There was very little furniture, so it was quite easy to use rooms for different activities. Gradually furniture became fussy and heavy, and as new houses were built they were designed with many rooms, each with a special use.

Homes today

Few people nowadays can afford houses with separate rooms for every purpose. Indeed, most people want their homes to be as easy and practical to live in as possible. Fewer and fewer people wish to spend a lot of time keeping house; they would rather use their house as a place of rest and relaxation.

An 18th-century town house

Glass windows

Bedroom

Servants' rooms

Sitting room

Main bedroom

Library

Drawing room

Dining room

Basement kitchen

Basement storeroom

Brick walls

▲ Town houses in the 18th century were often built tall and narrow in order to save space. Rooms stretched some way back from the street front, and they were piled one on top of another from basement kitchen to attic bedroom.

► Some people allow their houses to be taken over by animals and plants. In this house a special conservatory has been built on the back for the dog and plants.

Special homes

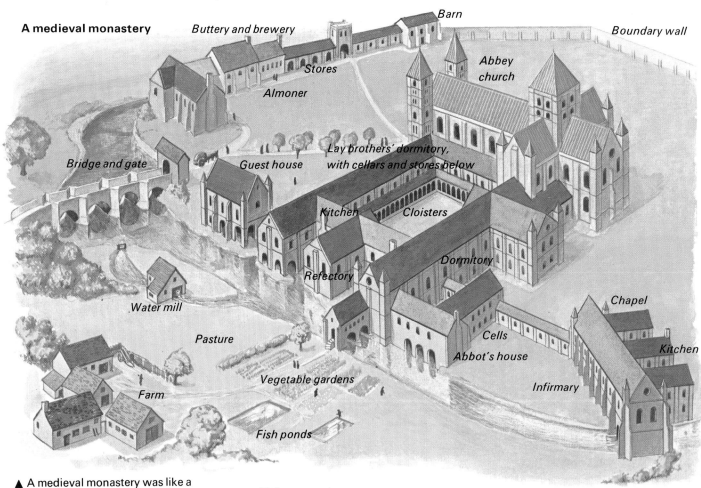

A medieval monastery

Buttery and brewery

Barn

Boundary wall

Stores

Almoner

Abbey church

Bridge and gate

Guest house

Lay brothers' dormitory, with cellars and stores below

Kitchen

Cloisters

Dormitory

Refectory

Water mill

Chapel

Pasture

Cells

Abbot's house

Kitchen

Farm

Vegetable gardens

Infirmary

Fish ponds

▲ A medieval monastery was like a village, in which the monks had everything they needed: their home, their food and their work. Some monasteries employed people from nearby villages to help them, but usually they were self-sufficient.

▼ An unusual monastery on the top of an enormously high cliff, Meteora in Greece houses a silent order of monks. Only men are allowed to enter the monastery, and they are hauled up the cliff in a basket.

▲ The Royal Hospital, Chelsea, is a famous home for old soldiers. All Chelsea Pensioners wear a special uniform. Each man has his own room, but they all eat in a central dining hall. They are better cared for like this than if they were living alone.

Adapted homes

Not everyone can choose where they want to live. Some people have jobs which mean living in a certain place. Some, such as the very old, cannot look after themselves, so they live with others who are in the same situation, in a home where they can receive the care and attention they need. Others, perhaps blind or disabled, live in houses that are basically ordinary, but which are adapted to their particular needs. When they have a house that suits them it is difficult for them to move away.

A house with the job

People who live in a building that goes with their work often do their best to make it comfortable and homely. For example, students moving into a hostel where all the rooms look alike put up posters and scatter books and records around. The rooms then feel different and look individual.

On the other hand, some houses that go with a job may not be altered. A beautiful home may be given to someone who holds a high post, in order to increase his prestige and underline the importance of his work. These houses must remain the same so that they can be recognized immediately by the public and respected as symbols of success in government or business. The residence of the president of the United States, the White House, has remained that colour since 1812. It helps to give a strong impression of the stability of government even though presidents come and go. The families of these important people must move into the official house and make it a home—but only for as long as the term of office.

▲ Living in a lighthouse presents special problems. They can be lonely places, far away from other people. As all the rooms are round it is hard to fit the furniture in. Eddystone lighthouse off the south coast of Britain has twice been destroyed by terrible storms, but today's lighthouse looks safe enough.

▼ All the chateaux in the wine-growing areas of France were specially built for making and storing wine. They all have large cellars where the wine is kept to mature.

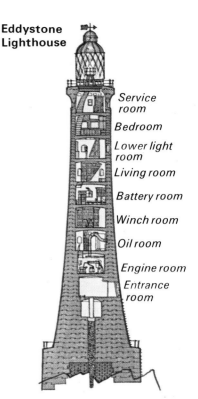

Eddystone Lighthouse

Service room
Bedroom
Lower light room
Living room
Battery room
Winch room
Oil room
Engine room
Entrance room

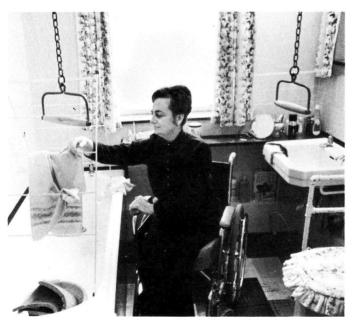

◄ Handicapped people need specially adapted homes. The pulley over the bath means that this woman can get in and out without any help.

► Doors are one of the biggest problems for people in wheelchairs. All the doors in this house slide so that they can be easily opened. Even spring-cleaning can be done from a wheelchair!

Disaster strikes

Natural disasters

However well a house is built, it is not always possible to avoid disaster. Some disasters may be fairly small like a fire, but even this can lead to loss of life. Others may be on a huge scale, leaving thousands of people homeless.

Sheltering people after a disaster is like building a city overnight. Absolutely everything has to be provided, from water supply and medicines to blankets, tents and clothing.

Earthquakes, tidal waves and hurricanes can destroy houses utterly. Scientists are developing warning systems, but none of these is yet totally effective. However effective they become, these warning systems may save people, but they will not save the normal house. Only houses specially built to withstand earthquakes and hurricanes will survive such disasters.

The west coast of the United States and Japan are both areas threatened by earthquakes where experimental shock-proof houses are being built. Houses built on a central pillar, rather like a tray balanced on one hand, should withstand the tremor, which will rock the house, but not bring it crashing to the ground.

Accidents do happen

Making sure that houses are safe is very important. Most countries have standards for fire safety and all new houses must satisfy them. For instance, electrical equipment must be installed correctly so that it is not dangerous. Other ways you can help prevent fires are to have flame-proofed curtains and night clothes, use fireguards in front of open fires, and turn pan handles inwards on the cooker.

▲ The Fire of London in 1666, painted by an unknown Dutch artist. This fire destroyed most of the timber-built houses of London, and the city had to be rebuilt.

▼ Fire is still a great hazard today, and no house is entirely free from fire risk.

◄ Although some areas are more prone to flooding than others, a combination of unusual weather conditions can often produce an unexpected flood. It will be quite a long time before these houses can be lived in again.

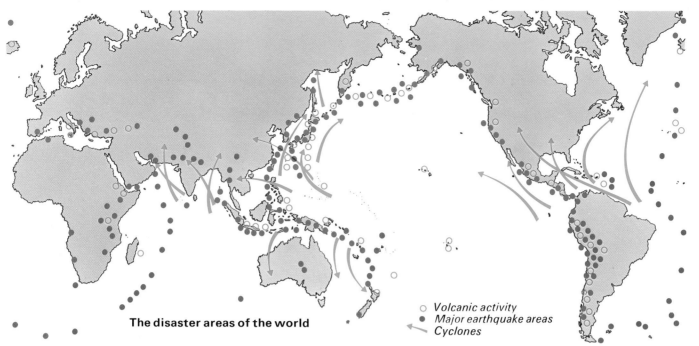

The disaster areas of the world

○ Volcanic activity
● Major earthquake areas
← Cyclones

▲ Earthquakes, volcanoes and typhoons only occur in specific areas, but no one yet knows how to predict when they will strike.

▲ An earth tremor in Yugoslavia caused the tower on this man's house to fall at his feet. A large tremor might have destroyed the whole street.

▶ The devastation caused by a cyclone in Darwin, Australia, December 1974. Nearly 40,000 people were made homeless.

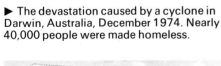

▲ A new house built in Darwin after the 1974 cyclone. The central pillars should help it to withstand another cyclone, by allowing the house to sway on its foundations.

21

Bad housing in growing cities

▶ This photograph of a London street at the turn of the century shows the number of families living in cramped and unhealthy conditions. The sun could not penetrate between the houses, and the central drainage gutter was smelly and unhygienic.

◀ A 19th-century courtyard. Rubbish dumps in the country rotted away, but in towns they became a quick way of spreading disease.

▼ *Industrial Landscape* by the English painter L. S. Lowry shows factories and houses crowded together in a smoky atmosphere.

What is a slum?

A single house may be dirty and badly built, but on its own it is not a slum. Slums happen when a whole district contains squalid houses, and when so many people live in them that the services to the houses are not adequate.

Early slums

In 19th-century Europe there was an enormous growth in the number of factories. Factory owners were looking for workers and generally paid higher wages than people could get for working on the land, so people flocked to the towns to find jobs. Houses were built near the factories. They were usually put up very quickly and made of poor materials without any of the water or drainage that was necessary. There were not enough houses so people who were desperate for work accepted very overcrowded conditions. It was not until there had been several terrible outbreaks of disease that the authorities began to provide services and set standards for house building.

The modern slum

It is much easier to understand how slums grow up than to solve the problem. People continue to crowd into the cities hoping to find work, especially in the developing countries. It is impossible to build enough houses for them all.

One solution to the problems of fast-growing towns is to provide at least the basic necessities. Some city authorities now provide water pipes in areas where people are likely to settle, and perhaps a bank of building materials and an advice centre. People are encouraged to build houses for themselves.

▲ Brasilia in Brazil is one of the world's newest cities, yet it still cannot house all its inhabitants. Beyond the great expanse of the shanty town you can see the tower blocks of the city.

◀ Two types of housing in Bombay. The terrible conditions in which some people have to live contrast starkly with the modern blocks of flats in the background.

▲ Even the best built and serviced homes can become slums when no one cares for the common areas like stairways and halls.

◀ In spite of having no permanent home this family has made the best of what they have. Their garden adds a degree of homeliness to their few possessions.

Planning an estate

▲ An aerial view of a village. It contains all the features essential to a community. The church in the centre is the focal point, with the shops, school and doctor nearby. People live near these central services and yet still within walking distance of their work in the fields. Many modern planners are trying to recapture the village atmosphere when building new estates.

Design for living

Building a new estate or a new town involves much more than rows and rows of houses. The most important factor is that people are going to live in those houses and must therefore be given all the facilities they need. The second most important factor is that the houses must be somewhere where people will want to live. It is no use building a new estate many miles from any work.

The people living in a new town will vary from single people, to families of four or five, to older people probably living alone. The houses and flats must therefore be of different sizes and designs to allow for this variation. Some planners think that it is better to mix these groups up, others that it is better to separate them. Once the number of houses and flats and the approximate number and type of people living in them has been established, the planners must think of the facilities needed.

What people need

A family with young children probably needs the greatest number of facilities. They require transport, shops, schools, parks, a health centre, and libraries. Other people would probably need at least some of these facilities. The planners have to be sure that the facilities are both adequate and not under-used. It would be very wasteful to build a school that was much too big for the community it served.

It would of course be possible to build houses with none of these facilities, but very few people would want to live in them, and those that did would find it very hard to make friends or to develop any feeling of belonging.

Planning

The lake on the left with an oil can floating in it was transformed into the estate shown below. This obviously took several years. The land had to be reclaimed and then allowed to settle before building could start. On the right is a plan of the estate. You can see that far more than just houses is included. Planning and designing an estate is a skilled job, requiring a great deal of imagination and attention to detail.

Planning for people's needs

School
For most families with young children a school nearby is an important consideration when choosing a house. Not only does this prevent a long and perhaps dangerous journey, it also helps the child to make friends with other children in the area.

Work
It is no use buying a house unless it is reasonably close to a place where jobs can be found. Most housing developments grow up around industrial areas or towns where shops and offices provide work.

Transport
Even though most families own cars it is still vital that housing developments have an efficient and reliable bus or train service. People can feel very isolated if it is difficult to travel to and from their homes.

Shops
Most people like to be within easy reach of a supermarket where they can do all their everyday food shopping under one roof. Many shopping centres today enable people to buy not only food but also clothes, household goods and books without stepping into the open.

Culture
People also like to live close to public libraries and social centres. Social centres are taking over from village halls as places where people can hold meetings, put on plays, go to evening classes, or meet for a chat.

Health
Health services are another important consideration. If people are ill they do not want to have to travel many miles to see a doctor. Dentists' surgeries, family planning clinics and baby clinics should also be close by.

Recreation
Few people today have large gardens so it is important to have recreation areas near houses where both children and adults can play games and sports or simply enjoy being in pleasant surroundings.

Planners have to think about all these things and more when they are designing a new housing development. If they do not provide the amenities that people have come to expect they will find it very difficult to attract buyers for their houses.

The design of a town

▲ The city wall of Avila in Spain was built to protect the city in the Middle Ages. Few cities today have their walls so well preserved. Parts of the walls of London, however, are still intact.

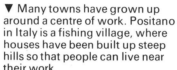

▼ Many towns have grown up around a centre of work. Positano in Italy is a fishing village, where houses have been built up steep hills so that people can live near their work.

An infinite variety

Houses in towns come in all shapes and sizes, and the towns themselves come in all shapes and sizes too. Some have grown naturally, round a castle for protection or a market for trade, with houses added here and there as needed.

Other towns have been planned from the beginning, perhaps to house the extra people from an overcrowded town. One very old, and very obvious, way to plan a town is to use a grid—a network of straight streets crossing one another at right angles to form blocks of houses. It was the standard pattern used by the Romans building new towns in remote parts of their empire. The grid system did not lose its popularity—New York has used it as well.

Transport

New forms of transport helped to produce a revolution in building materials, and they also greatly changed the shape of towns. With the development of trains it became possible for people to live a considerable distance from the centre of a town and yet travel in each day to work. New patterns of housing grew up in the suburbs, and are characteristic of towns today all over the world. At first they were built for people using trains; now they are designed for the car too.

The inner city

Once the centre of a town was its most bustling part because people lived close to their work. Many families lived in the rooms above a shop. Now it is more popular to live in the suburbs, so the inner city may be almost deserted by night, and peopled by day only by those who work there or come in to shop.

▲ One of the finest examples of 18th-century planning is the Royal Crescent in Bath. These houses were designed as a complete unit, part of a geometric plan, not as individual houses.

▼ The grid system often used in towns can look very stark from the air, but on the ground is probably quite pleasant. This estate in Australia has been designed as a pattern, but each house in it can be different.

▲ Ribbon development was never planned; it just happened. As new roads were built to factories and between towns, houses were slung along them with no thought given to amenities or services for the people living there. Today bypasses are allowing some to develop into real communities.

Problems for planners

Sometimes the original plans for houses are ruined by later developments. Motorways or the approach to airport runways can make life intolerable for people living nearby, but it is not always possible to provide them with another, quieter house.

High-rise living

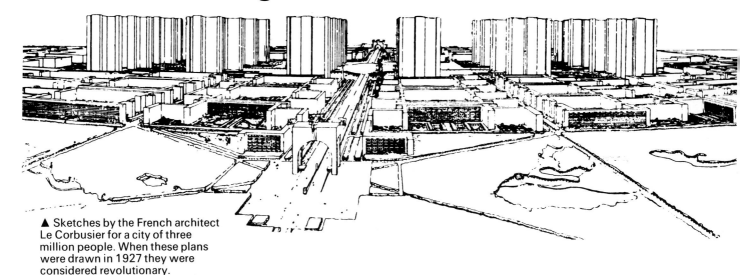

▲ Sketches by the French architect Le Corbusier for a city of three million people. When these plans were drawn in 1927 they were considered revolutionary.

▲ Goldberg's Marina City in Chicago, USA, bears a strong resemblance to a corn cob. Cars are parked at the bottom, offices are in the middle and flats on the top.

▶ Not all tower blocks are a success. These flats in St Louis, USA, have been blown up after vandalism made them impossible to live in.

A new form of housing

The one really new form of housing that has been built in the last thirty years is tower blocks. It is no new idea to live in a flat. Space in towns is limited, and if people want to live close to the centre and to their work it is sensible to stack their houses one on top of another. The novelty lies in making the blocks of flats so very large.

Two developments made the construction of huge blocks of flats possible: the discovery of new materials —plate glass, concrete and steel—and of new ways to build with them. In the early days of building upwards the new method was still very expensive, and "skyscrapers" were used only for offices. Firms could afford to pay the high rents needed to cover costs where families could not.

Living in a tower block

How did skyscrapers come to be used for housing? One reason is that building methods became more advanced and cheaper. A major factor in the expense of building houses is always the cost of men's wages. With the invention of huge cranes and other aids, it needed fewer men to build blocks of flats than were needed to build ordinary houses for the same number of people.

In its ideal form, living in a tower block can be convenient, with cheap heating and shops in the basement. But for some people the reality is very different from the architects' dreams. The flats in a block may have cramped rooms, so there is no space for children to play. If you don't know your neighbours, or if the lift breaks down, it is easy to feel trapped and lonely.

Where do they come from?

There are features on most houses that help you to recognize which country they are in, but these tower blocks could have been built anywhere. Can you guess which country each is in? The The answers are below.

▲ Looking out of the window from a flat in a tower block. From this height it is impossible to identify the people on the ground below, which can make you feel isolated from the rest of the world.

◀ Supplying central services to a tower block can cause problems. A minor gas explosion, for example, which at ground level may not be too serious, can have a fatal effect 25 floors up. Fire too is a greater danger in tall buildings.

▼ Lifts in some tower blocks have the buttons high up so that children cannot play with them. But supposing you live on the twentieth floor, how do you get up there if you can't reach the button?

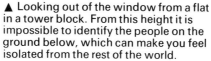

Answers: 1—Norway; 2—Australia; 3—France; 4—Canada.

29

Moveable homes

▲ The prosperous port of Hong Kong has attracted a large population looking for work. Many of these people have to live on temporary "sampans" in the harbour, supporting themselves by odd jobs and fishing.

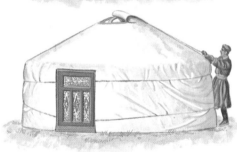

▼ The black tents of the Bedouin of the Sahara can vary considerably in size. A chieftain or "sheikh" may have several rooms inside his tent, divided from one another by curtains. The tents are always pitched so that the closed side faces the prevailing wind, in case of sandstorms.

► The Mongolian "yurt" can be carried on the backs of two camels, and assembled in half an hour. The framework is like a trellis; it is stretched out and the highly-decorated door put in position. The felt covering is then put over the framework. This covering is closely woven to keep out the cold of the Gobi desert.

Leading a mobile life

Whether through choice, chance or necessity, many people lead a mobile life. They may choose to see the world, taking a few years or a whole lifetime to observe how other people live. They may be driven out of their homes by the chance of war or by misfortune. They may be conforming to the way of life of their ancestors. But for people on the move, the shelter and security of a home are still necessary.

Nomads

Nomads are habitual wanderers who know no other way of life. The way of life of many nomads has evolved through centuries to fit the climate and the economic conditions of their native land. Many live in areas where there is low rainfall, or which can almost be classified as desert. As it is not possible to cultivate the ground, the nomads are herdsmen instead. When their animals have exhausted one patch of ground they must move on to another to graze.

Although this system has worked for centuries, in many places there is a great pressure on people who have led a semi-nomadic life to settle and cultivate the land. This is often because their migrations take them across political boundaries, much to the annoyance of the governments of those countries. The Eskimos, for example, are being encouraged to settle, as are many of the peoples of Africa. Nowadays it is only in the inhospitable desert that nomads are able to continue their traditional way of life without opposition.

Although we tend to think that only primitive peoples are nomadic, many people in the developed world uproot themselves regularly, often moving thousands of miles to be where their work is.

▲ Traditional gypsy caravans are not often seen now. But by passing traditions down to their children the customs of different people can be kept alive.

▼ The Lapps are semi-nomadic, often living by fishing in summer and only herding reindeer in the winter. Their tents are brightly decorated with traditional patterns.

Fantasy houses

◄ Do you ever dream of living in a golf ball? It seems unlikely, but a Frenchman designed this house in the 18th century, and probably the furniture to fit into it.

▼ If a moveable home is your dream, then this is probably for you. A group in San Francisco, USA, have converted a van into a real house on wheels.

Your dream house

Everyone has their own idea of the perfect place to live. For some it may be in a distant place far away from everyone and everything; others may long to live in the noise and bustle of a big town. It is nearly impossible to find your dream house unless you build it, since no one will have exactly the same ideas as you. In your own family, for example, you may find that you want a house with large bedrooms so that you can be independent, but your parents may want a large living room and small bedrooms.

You often read advertisements about the "dream kitchen". This usually means a kitchen with lots of labour-saving gadgets; to the overworked mother of a large family, this may indeed seem like the answer to her dreams.

Fantasies today

Nowadays it is less easy for even the most wealthy to indulge their building fantasies. Fantasy houses are often expensive, involving the use of skilled people and special materials. Local authorities also often prohibit house owners from making any unusual alterations or additions to their houses. The ornate and impractical houses and castles of two hundred years ago are definitely something of the past.

But although fantasy houses are a thing of the past, you can often see small signs of individuality on what at first appear to be quite ordinary houses. A concrete façade might be decorated in an unusual way, windows painted unexpectedly. It is worth looking out for these personal touches.

▼ On the Isle of Mull, off the coast of Scotland, you could hardly be further away from it all. To some people this is a dream come true.

▲ The owner of this house has indulged his fantasies fairly generously. His ordinary suburban house has been converted into a minor castle, complete with battlements. But the glass windows look rather out of place.

◄ The mock-classical Roman swimming pool of Hearst Castle in California, USA, is only a small part of the dream castle built by an American millionaire. Would you like to swim in it?

▲ This very ornate castle, Castle Neuschwanstein, was built by King Ludwig II of Bavaria in 1867. It was one of the magnificent castles built by the extravagant king before he was declared insane and forced to give up the throne.

▲ An ordinary block of flats in Barcelona, Spain, has been completely transformed by its windows. By introducing this small but striking change to a conventional design, Gaudi the architect has achieved an unusual effect.

▶ A house made of empty bottles, an original idea and also a practical one. The house would be warm and light, although the coloured bottles would keep some light out. Note also the decoration on the outside walls.

Learning from the past

▲ These few stones are all that is left of a Stone Age settlement, but even from this thin evidence experts can build up a general picture of how the people lived. It is possible to judge how many people might have lived here, how long ago, and the way they managed to feed themselves.

▲ People re-enacting life as it must have been during the Iron Age. They are basing their shelter, clothes and food on archaeological evidence. By trying to relive the Iron Age they can probably discover aspects of life in those times that would be difficult to imagine by ordinary study.

◄▼ From these two sources it is quite possible to reconstruct an ancient Egyptian house. The wall painting on the left shows clearly how the house was built, and the pottery model below gives a three-dimensional view of it. One of these pieces of evidence would provide an incomplete picture, but the two together help archaeologists to form an exact idea.

Houses as evidence

History is not just a matter of dates, recording great events. It is also the record of how people lived. Evidence of how people lived is left behind in their houses. Even if the houses have crumbled to dust the evidence is still there. Archaeologists carefully dig up the places inhabited by earlier people, and can interpret the tiny pieces of evidence found there. Food remains from a rubbish pit, or broken pots, are enough to give the archaeologist an idea of how someone lived.

People built houses and lived an organized existence for a long while before writing was widespread. Even after writing had been invented very few ordinary people used it. It was only the political and religious events of great importance that were recorded. It is therefore necessary to look elsewhere to find out about the daily life of ancient peoples. This is exactly how the researches of archaeologists are used.

Climate and materials

Archaeological sites vary from piles of stones to perfectly preserved houses. It is often the climate and building materials that determine whether a house survives or not. Large fragments of Roman cities have been preserved in the warm climate of the Mediterranean, so that it is possible to reconstruct the daily life of the Romans in some detail. The Roman city of Pompeii, which was buried under lava during an eruption of the volcano Vesuvius in AD 79, was uncovered centuries later almost intact.

On the other hand, far less is known of the daily life of the Vikings because their houses were probably built of wood and turf, which has rotted away over the centuries.

▲ A reconstruction of a Red Indian compound near Lake Huron in Canada. The original compound rotted away as it was only made from wood and bark, but from other sources archaeologists have reconstructed how they think it would have looked. As these compounds are not very old some of the evidence for them may have come from surviving descendants of the original Indians.

▼ The Romans are famous for their original and successful method of central heating. Evidence for Roman central heating has been found in several places in Britain. The floors of rooms were built on supports, around which hot air from a nearby furnace circulated. This hot air warmed the floor, and as a result, heated the rest of the room.

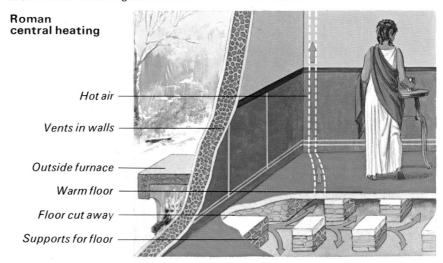

Roman central heating

Hot air

Vents in walls

Outside furnace

Warm floor

Floor cut away

Supports for floor

▼ A reconstruction of Fishbourne Palace in Britain, made entirely from archaeological evidence. The palace was built by a rich Roman citizen in about AD 75.

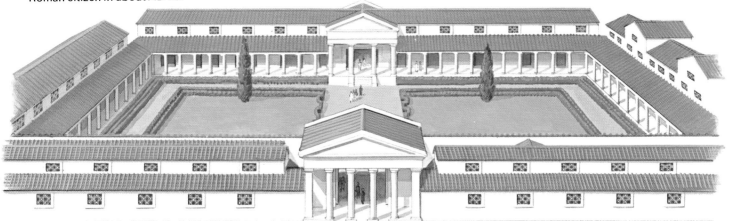

Houses as museums

▲ These Bulgarian houses have been restored in traditional style. The original houses were made of carved wood with intricate decoration. These have now been restored and will be preserved. In this way people will be able to learn about the craftsmanship of their ancestors.

◀ The centre of Warsaw in Poland was completely destroyed by bombs during World War II. After the war the people of Warsaw wanted to see their city restored to its former glory. Basing their plans on an old painting, they rebuilt the city centre exactly as it used to be. It is hard to realize that these houses were built only twenty years ago.

◀ The places where famous people live are often preserved as museums. George Washington, the first President of the USA, lived in this house in Virginia. Every year thousands of people visit it and see how Washington and his family lived.

Why conserve houses?

Many of the houses in towns and villages all over the world are old ones, and some of them are no longer as suitable as they once were for the kind of life people live today. Yet many old houses are still carefully looked after. There are several reasons for keeping these houses rather than knocking them down and starting again.

One reason is that some older houses provide examples of old skills that have been lost since traditional methods and materials gave way to new. Another is that although some houses may be too large or too inconvenient to live in, they are considered so beautiful or so historically interesting that it is worth preserving them. One way of doing this is for several families to live in the house by converting it into flats, or for one family to live in part of the house and open the rest of it to the public. Keeping the house in good repair can be very expensive and the visitors pay towards the upkeep.

Groups of houses

Some old houses are not particularly interesting in themselves, but their value comes from their situation, their relationship with other houses. If you think of a town or village made completely of new houses and one with both new and old houses mixed together, almost certainly the town with a mix of old and new will look more interesting. It may have unexpected views down a side-street, or small shops as well as the newer chain stores. Many countries now have laws to protect the older houses in historic towns from being swept away to make space for shopping centres, office blocks and other new developments.

▲ All the rooms in the stately homes of the past are of interest. The left-hand picture shows one room being used for its original purpose—a large reception. The kitchen on the right has been kept with all its old equipment.

Homes of the past
It is not just the houses of the famous that are preserved. The homes of very ordinary people can tell us a great deal about the past. Some have been turned into museums, but many others are still lived in.

A Norwegian timber and turf house of 1500

A Dutch house of 1500

A yeoman's house of 1500 in southern England

The changing interior

▲ This bleak castle must have been very cold to live in ! Five hundred years ago there were very few comforts inside houses. Even today with central heating it would not be easy to keep warm.

▲ Very rich people are able to decorate the inside of their houses in a unique way. It is difficult to assess how many people must have been involved in the decoration of this room in the Palace of Fontainebleau, France.

▼ This 19th-century drawing room provides a striking contrast to the castle above. Every possible space is filled with curtains, drapes and ornaments, so there is hardly room to sit down.

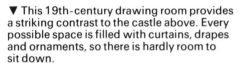

▲ This modern room does not look much like many of our homes, but probably all our homes have an element of this room in them. The colours are bright, the furniture sparse and the comfort considerable. The invention of plate glass has made it possible to have much larger windows than before.

Fireplaces

A medieval stone fireplace

An ornate 19th-century fireplace in the style of Louis XV

Fireplaces have changed considerably over the centuries. They first started as a pile of fuel burning in the middle of the room, with the smoke rising through a hole in the roof. A fireplace at the side of the room with a chimney was the next development, with a succession of designs for the fireplace itself. Today we often have no fireplace at all, simply a radiator for heating.

A 19th-century fireplace

Personal taste

The decoration and appearance of the inside of a house is very much a matter of personal taste, but this is always influenced by fashion, availability of materials and craftsmen, and expense. Hundreds of years ago most houses were plain and simple. Gradually they became more ornate, even the poorest of houses having some form of decoration. Houses today tend once again to be very simple, while retaining the luxuries and comforts not available to our ancestors.

Most people, when they move into a new house, gradually redecorate the interior. People's ideas about decoration vary a lot. Some may like ornate wallpaper, others plain, white walls; some may like highly patterned curtains and furnishings, others only very simple furniture and decorations to give rooms an uncluttered look.

Different countries, different styles

It is interesting that even today when so many things are shared and exchanged between countries, the styles of decoration in a home remain very national. It is unusual to see shutters or blinds in a British house, and it is equally unusual to see curtains in a German house. In Italy very few homes have carpets, the floors being mainly of stone with rugs, whereas in northern Europe carpets are more usual, principally because of the cold. Colours also tend to vary from country to country. In very hot countries the insides of houses are often pale and cool-looking, whereas in colder countries colours tend to be brighter to give a feeling of warmth.

The comparison between the insides of people's homes is endless. Just to compare your house with your next door neighbour's would reveal many differences.

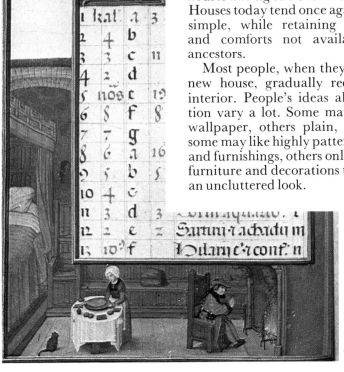

▲ ► Bedrooms have changed a great deal over the last five hundred years in both comfort and function. Five hundred years ago, most bedrooms had a large fire, a four-poster bed with curtains, making the bed like a small room, and very little else. Today bedrooms are lighter and airier, and often used as living rooms as well as bedrooms.

Outside appearances

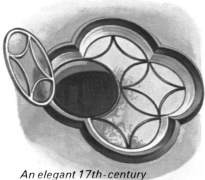

An elegant 17th-century country house window

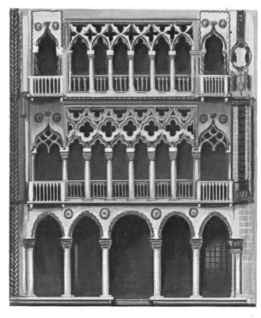

A Venetian stone balcony

▲ ▶A varied selection of windows and balconies.

A 17th-century iron balcony

The importance of decoration

The appearance of a house is determined by several influences. One important one is climate, which may influence the shape, another is the materials and craftsmanship of the building. Yet it is not these important influences but the decoration on the outside of the house which is its most immediately noticeable feature.

The decoration of a house is partly a matter of fashion—houses can be designed in the latest style just as clothes can. But there may be other good reasons for the way a house is decorated. Paint can be used to make an effect quite cheaply. For instance, if all the houses in a street are painted the same colour, the street may look more imposing. On the other hand, the people who live in a house may want to tell the world that they are different from their neighbours, and painting their house an unlikely colour is one way of doing it.

Decoration or design?

The separate parts of a house can be used to add to the external effect. Doors, windows and other features can be made to a traditional pattern with each one differing only slightly from the next. Sometimes each separate part is designed to fit in with the rest, so that each detail adds to the total effect. All this is the job of the architect, who has to make sure the house looks good as well as fitting the needs of the people who are to live in it.

▲ Chimneys are often an excellent opportunity for bricklayers to reveal their skills. The brickwork on these two 16th-century chimney-stacks is complicated but very attractive.

▶ It is often the doors and gates that make each house unique.

Late 18th-century door

Late 18th-century iron gate

▲ The mud from which this Moroccan house was made has also been used as decoration. The mud was moulded when the house was built, and has lasted since then.

▲ Many houses in Germany, Switzerland and Austria are beautifully painted and decorated with carved wood. This house is in Bavaria, Germany.

▶ Enlivening a tower block. This tower block in England has been decorated with abstract patterns to make the block look less grim and to break the effect of a great mass of concrete.

▼ These gaily painted houses are in Pretoria, South Africa. Some of the designs may originally have been intended to ward off evil spirits.

The house of the future

▲ A house consisting of a series of domes made out of old car panels. Buckminster Fuller, a famous American architect, studied the possibilities of living in domes and decided it was one of the most economical methods of housing.

◄ Fitting solar panels to heat water and provide central heating is comparatively easy. This ordinary house has had a black corrugated panel covered with glass built into the roof. Water runs over the panel and under the glass and is heated by the sun. The hot water runs through a pipe in the water tank and heats the rest of the water. The same water is then pumped back to the roof to be heated again by the sun. Even with very little sun this is an effective way of heating your water. But although once the solar panels are installed, hot water can be obtained for free, the cost of fitting them is still fairly high.

Plug-in living

The common idea of the house of the future used to be a dream of plug-in living. Almost everything was done by electricity and every conceivable kind of machine was available to help humans with everything from making the beds to building a new house in a very few hours. The resources crisis has changed all that. We must now find ways of conserving the energy we have, or look for alternative sources of power.

Conserving energy

Building new houses specially designed to conserve energy would seem to be the ideal solution. But no country could afford to provide new houses for everyone. The cost of materials and labour, let alone of destroying existing houses to build new ones, would just be too high. So we have to make do with the houses we have, but think of ways of using less energy to heat and service them. Insulating houses, for example, helps to keep them warm without having a fire or central heating on all the time.

Alternative energy

Coal, oil and gas used to be relatively cheap sources of fuel, but they are becoming more expensive to extract from the ground and supplies are running out. So we must look for other ways of producing power. One idea is for houses to be self-sufficient in energy, that is for each house to use the sun's rays, the wind and domestic waste to produce enough energy for its own heat and light. But people will continue to live in cities because populations are so large, so we must also look at alternative sources of energy for houses that have no spare land around them.

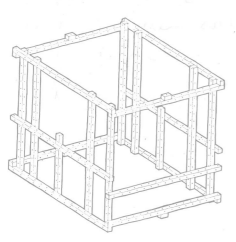

◄► A living room of the future? You could convert your bedroom so that it has only this "module", on which you sleep, work and keep your belongings. It is made of lots of pieces of wood screwed together in the combination that suits you best. All the pieces of wood have a number of screw holes so that you can change the height of a particular level. This "module" means that you have lots of extra space in the rest of the room.

A self-sufficient house

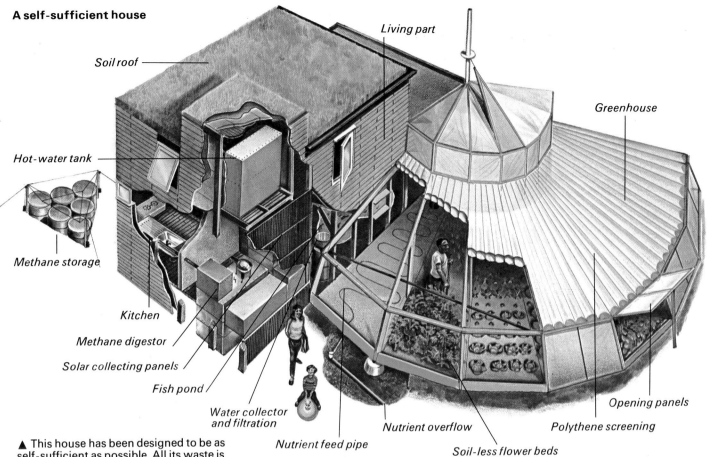

Living part

Soil roof

Greenhouse

Hot-water tank

Methane storage

Kitchen

Methane digestor

Solar collecting panels

Fish pond

Water collector and filtration

Nutrient feed pipe

Nutrient overflow

Soil-less flower beds

Opening panels

Polythene screening

▲ This house has been designed to be as self-sufficient as possible. All its waste is recycled and is used as gas for cooking and heating. All the food is grown in the greenhouse and the house itself is insulated against the cold by turf on the roof and wooden walls. This design is similar to the Scandinavian houses on page 9. The main disadvantage of a house like this is the amount of land that it needs.

◄ People have experimented with living underwater. As with living in the Antarctic there are science research stations underwater, but no one has actually made a home there. The main problem is the huge pressure deep in the sea, and the fact that the deeper you go the darker it gets. There is, however, the advantage of a plentiful food supply.

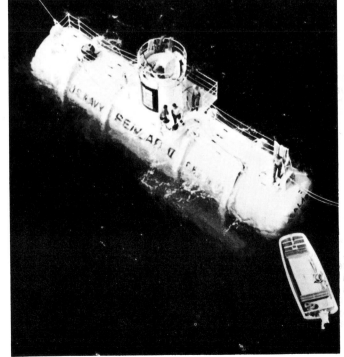

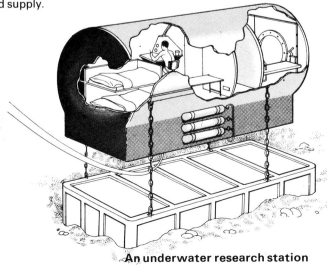

An underwater research station

Project an architect's job

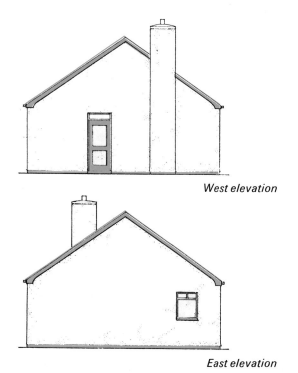

West elevation

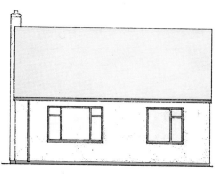

South elevation

East elevation

North elevation

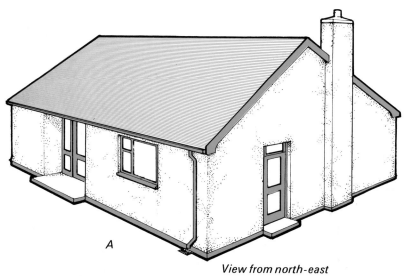

A

View from north-east

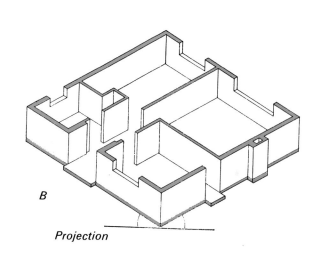

B

Projection

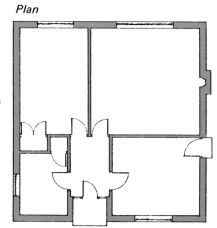

Plan

Designing a house

Even the simplest houses have to have working drawings so that they can be translated from an idea in the mind of the architect to a real building on the ground. The diagrams on this page show how the various parts of a building can be expressed on paper.

When a customer first asks an architect to design a house he will have certain ideas he wants the architect to use in his overall design. The architect produces working drawings so that both he and the client can see how the house is shaping up.

He will produce views of the house with each side straight on. These are called

elevations and show where doors and windows come on the outside. *Projections* show how the various parts of a house fit together. Drawing A is a view of the house as you might see it when walking round the outside and diagram B is a cut-away projection of the same view showing the hidden interior.

Plans show how rooms fit together inside the house, seen looking straight down from above. These are important for the builder as all the practical details he needs to do the work are marked on them, such as measurements and position of pipes and electric points.

Make a survey of your room

To make a plan of your room you first need to choose a scale. A practical one for most people is 1:100 (1 centimetre on paper represents 100 centimetres on the ground). It usually helps to use squared paper. Mark in the position of furniture and cupboards as well as the fittings shown on the list above. Remember to show how much space needs to be allowed for opening doors and windows without hitting the furniture, and make sure your diagram shows them opening in the right direction.

View of living room

Drawing to scale

Everything on an architect's drawing has to be drawn accurately to scale so that it is shown taking up the amount of space it really does. The scale of each drawing is marked on it. Different scales can show plans in varying amounts of detail.

▼ A more detailed plan by an architect of the house on the left-hand page, showing the positions of the fittings and furnishings. By referring to the architects' symbols (below left), you can see where the switches, light fittings and plugs are situated. The blue curved lines show how much space the doors take up when they are opened and shut. Look particularly closely at the plan of the living room and compare it with the illustration of the same room above.

Plan: approximate scale 1:5

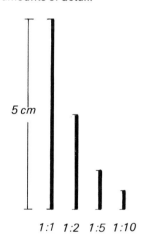

5 cm

1:1 1:2 1:5 1:10

Symbols

Architects' symbols are internationally approved so your diagram should be understood in other countries too.

- Electric socket outlet
- Electric cooker outlet
- One-way light switch
- Two-way light switch
- Pendant light fitting
- Immersion heater switch
- Telephone point

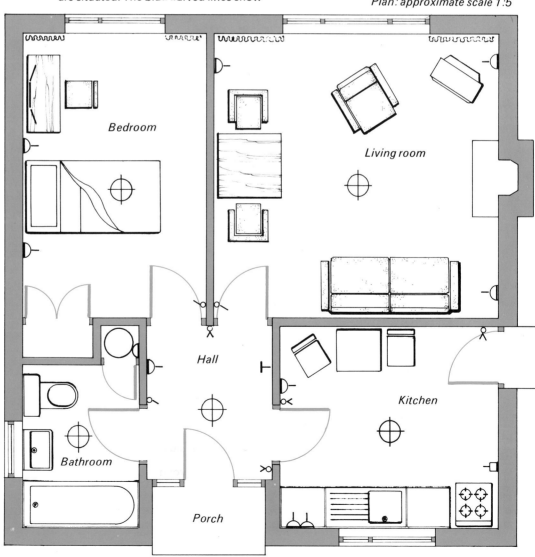

Bedroom

Living room

Hall

Bathroom

Kitchen

Porch

Reference

Books to read

General

Observer Book of Architecture helps to identify the different periods in architecture.

Pillar to Post and *Home Sweet Home* by Osbert Lancaster (John Murray). An entertaining and informative look at the design of houses through the ages and how people lived in them.

Houses by M. and A. Potter (John Murray). Explains how an architect sees houses old and new.

Specific subjects

Your House, the Outside View by John Prizeman (Hutchinson).

Architecture Without Architects by Bernard Rudofsky (Doubleday). Do-it-yourself housing from all over the world.

Buildings and Building Sites by Eric Jones (Batsford). Building techniques.

Shelter by Nan Fairbrother (Penguin Connexions). Why do we need houses?

Architecture 2000 by Charles Jencks (Studio Vista). Some ideas for the future.

The Buildings of England by Niklaus Pevsner (Penguin). Gives the historical background for buildings all over England (Wales, Ireland to follow). Look up the houses in your town.

Keep the Home Fires Burning, about fire and fireplaces, and *Clean and Decent* about bathrooms and sanitation. By Lawrence Wright (Routledge & Kegan Paul).

A History of Building Materials by Norman Davey (Phoenix House). Unusual ones are included.

History of the House ed. E. Camesasca (William Collins). Examines different periods in detail.

House and Garden Book of Interior Decoration (Conde Nast Publications).

Glossary

Architect Someone who designs and plans buildings, and is responsible for the supervision of their construction.

Development Term used to describe a newly-built collection of houses, designed to form a group.

Façade The face of a building, usually its principal front and the one which is most imposing.

Frame System for building some houses of timber or concrete. Posts bear the loads and walls are fitted in afterwards.

Insulation Surrounding walls or lining a roof with material that does not conduct heat easily, to keep interiors warm.

Louvre A blind made of overlapping struts, which allows air but not light through.

Membrane A thin pliable sheet, often of black polythene, which does not allow damp through. Placed between two courses of bricks on outside walls.

Planner Someone who decides where houses are to be built, bearing in mind the needs of the community for shops and services.

Plumber Someone who connects the water system in a house. From the French 'plomb' (lead) because pipes were originally made of lead.

Prefabricated Parts of a house made in a factory. They are assembled on the building site.

Services Include water, heating, transport, shops, refuse collection. They supply the needs of people living in one particular place.

Settlement A small village or collection of houses. Often used to describe a village that has later disappeared.

Shanty town Town that has grown so fast that it cannot house its inhabitants in proper buildings. Most people live in temporary shacks with few services.

Stonemason One who is skilled in a craft connected with stone—cutting it out of the ground, 'dressing' it in regular blocks, or carving or building with it.

Suburb Outlying district of a town which can only be reached from the town centre by a considerable journey.

Tower block Large block of flats, usually of 20 floors or over, and made with prefabricated parts.

Trellis Structure of wooden bars crossing each other at intervals, leaving spaces in between. Can be collapsible.

Ventilation The means by which a supply of fresh air is brought into a house.

What to look out for

When you start looking at houses really hard you may begin to see all sorts of little differences in them that you never realized existed. We often think that each house in a road is identical to its neighbour. But walk along the road comparing the windows in each house you pass, or the doors, or the garden gates. You will soon see that an enormous amount of care has gone into producing the variety.

Places to visit

However you will want to see unusual houses too. The National Trust owns many that are beautiful or historically interesting, and it is possible to go and visit them. You can also join the National Trust if you want to help with the valuable work of conservation that they do. The address is: The National Trust, Junior Division, The Old Grape House, Cliveden, Maidenhead, Berkshire. (The sister organization for Scotland is the National Trust for Scotland.)

Houses that have been preserved in an open-air museum can be seen at the Avoncroft Museum of Buildings, near Bromsgrove, Worcestershire.

The Civic Trust, 17 Carlton House Terrace, London SW1 works towards the conservation of houses in towns, while Europa Nostra at the same address aims to do this all over Europe.

The Commonwealth Institute, Kensington High Street, London W8 has examples of the ways in which people live in many parts of the world.

There are many houses currently being built to save energy—the progress of one has been monitored and shown by a television company. More information can be obtained from the Conservation Society, 12 London Street, Chertsey, Surrey KT16 8AA.

One charity, Shelter, 86 Strand, London WC2, exists to give help and advice to those who are homeless. It is always ready to explain the problems of housing and has produced some excellent kits and publications.

The Victoria and Albert Museum, Exhibition Road, London SW7 has several galleries of interiors of houses, showing furniture and decorations in a historical context. Old paintings, too, often portray fascinating details of the way people lived in the past.

Index

Illustration credits
Key to the position of illustrations: (T) top, (C) centre, (B) bottom and combinations; for example (TR) top right, or (CL) centre left.

Photographs
Aerofilms: 24(TL), 27(TR)
Paul Almasy: 16(BL)
Alpha: 33(C)
Architectural Association: 28(BR), 42(T)
Associated Press: 21(C), 27(BR)
Australian News and Information Bureau: 6(B), 9(BL), 20(BL), 21(BL), 21(BR), 27(C), 29
Barnabys: 33(BR), 38(BR)
Nick Birch: 23(BR), 29(TL)
Bodleian Library: 39(BL)
Bovis: 24(BR, BL)
British Antarctic Survey: 7(B)
British Museum: 34(B)
Camera and Pen: 18(BR), 23(T), 26(B), 27(TL), 36(B), 41(BL)
Canadian National Film Board: 35(T)
Canadian Tourist Office: 29, 35
Ron Chapman: 4(B)
Le Corbusier: 28(T)
Daily Telegraph: 37(TL), 40(C)
Dutch Embassy: 12(BL)
Mark Edwards: 19(BR, BL), 29(BC)
Werner Forman: 8(BR)
French Tourist Office: 19(C), 29
GLC: 22(TR)

Richard and Sally Greenhill: 31(T)
Peter W Haebertin: 3
Sonia Halliday: 10
Robert Harding Associates: 6(TR), 28(L)
Ikon: 7(T), 14(T), 27(BL)
Japanese Embassy: 16(BC)
Osbert Lancaster: 29(BL)
Manchester Evening News: 13(BL)
Margaret Murray: 8(T), 8(BL), 16(BR), 23(C), 23(BL), 34(TR)
National Trust: 37(TR)
Norwegian Embassy: 9(BR), 29
Picturepoint: 4(T), 5(TR), 6(TL), 12(BR), 19(T), 20(T), 32(C), 32(B), 33(TR), 33(BL), 34(TL), 36(C), 38(TL), 41(TL), 41(BR)
Poggenpohl: 14(B)
Popperfoto: 26(T)
Radio Times Hulton Picture Library: 38(BL)
Tate Gallery: 22(B)
Thelwell: 13(BR)
UNESCO Courier: 36(TR, TL)
Elizabeth Whiting: 17, 39(BR)
ZEFA: 5(TL), 18(BL), 20(BL), 30(T), 31(B), 38(TR), 41(TR)

Artists
Peter Connolly: 30-31, 35
Chris Forsey: 9, 16, 17
Ron Hayward Art Group: 3, 5, 6, 7, 10, 11, 12, 13, 43
Tony Payne: 11, 18, 19, 39, 40